FLANDERS' BOOK OF FAITH

THE SIMPSONS™ LIBRARY OF WISDOM
FLANDERS' BOOK OF FAITH

HarperCollins*Publishers*
77—85 Fulham Palace Road
Hammersmith, London W6 8JB
www.harpercollins.co.uk

Published by HarperCollins 2008

FIRST EDITION
ISBN-13: 978-0-00-726709-5

ISBN-10: 0-00-726709-6

3 5 7 9 10 8 6 4 2

Publisher: Matt Groening
Creative Director: Bill Morrison
Managing Editor: Terry Delegeane
Director of Operations: Robert Zaugh
Art Director: Nathan Kane
Special Projects Art Director: Serban Cristescu
Production Manager: Christopher Ungar
Assistant Art Director: Chia-Hsien Jason Ho
Production/Design: Karen Bates, Art Villanueva
Staff Artists: Mike Rote
Production Assistant: Nathan Hamill
Administration: Sherri Smith
Legal Guardian: Susan A. Grode

THE SIMPSONS™ LIBRARY OF WISDOM

Conceived and Edited by Bill Morrison
Book Design, Art Direction, and Production by Serban Cristescu
Contributing Editor: Terry Delegeane

HarperCollins Editors: Hope Innelli and Jeremy Cesarec

Contributing Artists: EDWIN AGUILAR, MARCOS ASPREC, KAREN BATES, DARREL BOWEN,
JOHN COSTANZA, SERBAN CRISTESCU, DAN DAVIS, MIKE DECARLO, SCOTT MCRAE, JEANETTE MORENO,
BILL MORRISON, KIMBERLY NARSETE, KEVIN M. NEWMAN, KEVIN ROTE, MIKE ROTE, KEVIN SEGNA,
ROBERT STANLEY, ERICK TRAN, ART VILLANUEVA

Contributing Writers: MARY TRAINOR, SCOTT M. GIMPLE, BILL MORRISON, TOM PEYER

Special Thanks to: Pete Benson, N. Vyolet Diaz, Deanna MacLellan, Helio Salvatierra, Mili Smythe, and Ursula Wendel

FLANDERS' BOOK OF FAITH

HARPER

NEW YORK • LONDON • TORONTO • SYDNEY

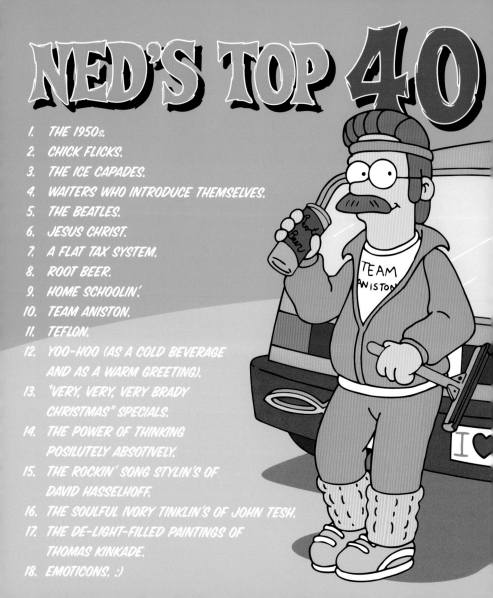

NED'S TOP 40

1. THE 1950s.
2. CHICK FLICKS.
3. THE ICE CAPADES.
4. WAITERS WHO INTRODUCE THEMSELVES.
5. THE BEATLES.
6. JESUS CHRIST.
7. A FLAT TAX SYSTEM.
8. ROOT BEER.
9. HOME SCHOOLIN'.
10. TEAM ANISTON.
11. TEFLON.
12. YOO-HOO (AS A COLD BEVERAGE AND AS A WARM GREETING).
13. "VERY, VERY, VERY BRADY CHRISTMAS" SPECIALS.
14. THE POWER OF THINKING POSILUTELY ABSOTIVELY.
15. THE ROCKIN' SONG STYLIN'S OF DAVID HASSELHOFF.
16. THE SOULFUL IVORY TINKLIN'S OF JOHN TESH.
17. THE DE-LIGHT-FILLED PAINTINGS OF THOMAS KINKADE.
18. EMOTICONS. :)

19. McJOBS.
20. MAGNETIC RIBBONS ON CARS.
21. RAPTURE-READY TOTE BAGS.
22. MAUDE'S MEATLOAF (MAY IT REST IN PEACE).
23. THE SPRINGFIELD DINNER THEATRE'S SAMUEL BECKETT FESTIVAL.
24. LIMITED EDITION COMMEMORATIVE PORCELAIN PLATES OF PRINCESS DIANA.
25. JAZZERCISE.
26. FIRE.
27. BRIMSTONE.
28. ERNEST BORGNINE.
29. BOB SAGET.
30. THEME RESTAURANTS.
31. THE CLASSIC CONTOURS OF THE 1992 GEO METRO.
32. THINKIN' INSIDE THE BOX.
33. VOTIN' MY VALUES.
34. STAYIN' THE COURSE.
35. A CLEAN WINDSHIELD.
36. EASY LISTENIN' SOFT-ROCK RADIO.
37. PANTS WITH JUST A SKOSH MORE ROOM IN THE SEAT.
38. THE DVD BOX SET OF "THE GOLDEN GIRLS" (SEASONS 1-6).
39. THAT COZY WAY MY JOGGING SUIT FEELS WHEN IT'S FRESH FROM THE DRYER.
40. FEELIN' GROOVY.

Focus on the Flanders Family Tree

LADY NEDEBEL FLANDERS

LORD NOSE

NEDMOND FLANDERS

WILHELMINA DÜMPERDORF

begat

NEDGAR "NE'ER-DO-WELL" FLANDERS

SOME TRAMP HE MET IN ST. LOUIS

JEHOSHAPHAT "JOSE" FLANDERS

FLORADORA FLANNERY

begat

NEDWARD FLANDERS (BACHELOR)

NEDSEL "DADDIO" FLANDERS

begat

AGNES "KOOKIE" TURNIPSEED

THE FLANDERS THAT FLOUNDERED

NEDIANA FLANDERS (D-I-V-O-R-C-E-D)

ASK-AROONIE *the* NEDSTER!

WELL, *HOWDY* AND *WELCOME* TO GOD'S LITTLE CORNER, KIDIDDLES! NOW, WHO'S GOT A *Q* IN NEED OF AN *A*?

WHO'S *GOD*?

I KNOW! I KNOW! GOD IS *LOVE*!

ROGER DODGER, MILHOUSE. GOD *IS* LOVE.

IF GOD IS *LOVE*, WHY DOES HE SEND PEOPLE TO *HELL*?

WELL... ¦HEE, HEE¦ TECHNICALLY *GOD* DOESN'T SEND ANYONE TO HELL, LISA.

PEOPLE SEND *THEMSELVES* THERE. IT'S WHAT WE CALL "FREE WILL."

I THOUGHT "FREE WILL" WAS A *WHALE*.

MAYBE "FREE WILL" WAS THE WHALE THAT ATE JONAH.

Ned Answers Kids' Questions About Religion

NED'S DAILY-DIDDLY DIARY!

5:30 AM: Woke up, did my "Pray Before Day."

5:50 AM: Worked out: 120 squat thrusts, bridge-ups, kettlebell jerks, shin kickers, bicepticons, inverse curl inchworms, chimney sweeps, rope-a-popes, shake-n-bakes, and tootsie touchers.

6:50 AM: Made breakfast for the boys: oatmeal (thinned with water, not milk) served with crackers and dry white toast.

7:50 AM: Drove boys to school, listenin' to "Mornin' Glory with Goopy and Morrie" on 102.7 BLISS FM.

8:30 AM: Picked up trash in Springfield Park, shined statue of Jebediah Springfield, then stood on corner of Main and Elm in case anyone needed directions.

9:30 AM: Arrived at the mall. Had a cup of hot water with Bagda, the proprietor of Global Shawarmin'.

10 AM: Opened the Leftorium for business. Set up display for left-handed mousepad sale. Discounted left-handed canoe paddles. Had a customer! Sold a left-handed weed whacker to a Canadian landscaper who lost his right arm in a topiary accident.

1 PM: Closed store for a 20-minute lunch. Ate at the new, low-salt, fast food stall in the food court, Bland on the Run.

1:20 PM: Reopened store and made a sale. A "My Left Foot" DVD! Brainstormed on a new campaign to expand the ol' consumer base: "Get Ambidextrous! Be MORE than right!"

4 PM: Met Reverend Lovejoy for crisis counseling after dropping a left-handed bowling ball on my foot and cussing. The Reverend assured me "snickerdoodle" isn't a curse. Still feel guilty, though.

5 PM: Started making dinner: boiled potato sandwiches on white with a bowl of melted butter for dippin'.

5:30 to 6 PM: Said grace.

6 PM: Dinner.

7 PM: Cleaned up with the boys while we listed all the things we're grateful for. Oh, that Todd...he said he was "grateful for being able to be grateful!"

7:30 PM: Read Rod and Todd my fan-fic novel "Harry Potter and the Consequences of Dabbling in Magic." Then put them to bed.

8:30 PM: Did my "Pray at End of Day." Remembered what Todd said about being grateful for being able to be grateful and cried some tears of gratitude, being careful to blow the ol' honker quietly so as not to wake the boys. Counted my blessings. Got to #143 (not being lactose intolerant) before drifting off to Dreamland.

11:27 PM: Heard someone outside my door and found Homer lying on my stoop, singing about how he "can't drive fifty five." Saw his car was parked in my tulip garden, still running and filled with stolen pizzas. (First clue: I couldn't find a receipt. Second clue: Homer kept shouting, "I stole them pizzas good!") Parked his car in the Simpson driveway, carried Homer home, and returned pizzas to Luigi's.

12 AM: Finally got back to bed. Fell asleep realizing I smelled like a giant pepperoni. Knowing I could smell worse, I was even grateful for that.

MAUDE FLANDERS LATE MATE AND MOTHER OF NED'S LITTLE KIDIDDLES

Maude Flanders was Ned's soulmate, helpmate, roommate, and—when necessary—playmate. They agreed on everything, from the sinfulness of pop culture to the sinfulness of fine art. When the Lord took her from Ned and the boys in a tragic FASCAR Fan-Demonium T-shirt accident, Reverend Lovejoy's eulogy summed up her life touchingly: "In many ways, Maude Flanders was a supporting player in our lives. She didn't grab our attention with memorable catchphrases, or comical accents. But, whether you noticed her or not, Maude was always there...and we thought she always would be."

● Quote: "I don't judge Homer and Marge.
   That's for a vengeful God to do."

● Education: Maude once attended a Bible camp to learn to be more judgmental.

● Liked: Unflavored ice milk, ficus plants, "Newsweek," being just a little sexy (but not around Homer).

● Disliked: Cartoon violence, liberal education, sugar, and anything else that might stimulate defenseless children.

● Faults: Sometimes Maude outlined passages in Ned's Bible because she couldn't find hers. Also, she once hired Japanese mobsters to intervene when Marge Simpson's pretzel operation threatened her pita business.

● Thing we don't talk about: The accident that caused her untimely passing was pretty much Homer Simpson's fault.

● Legacy: Ned fulfilled his late wife's dream to open the Christian-themed amusement park Praiseland. The plaque at the base of her statue there reads: "She taught us the joy of shame and the shame of joy."

Ned protects his sons from the outside world's devilish influences, especially "the two major temptations in life: girls and rock 'n' roll music." He has already taught them a deep love for the Bible and a crippling fear of bugs. Rod, the older of the two, enjoys praying and playing wholesomely with his brother. Impressionable Todd can get hostile and aggressive when he eats sugar or hears swearing.

- Quotes:
  ROD: "Oh, boy! Liver!"
  TODD: "Iron helps us play!"

- Rod can be found: Being quiet during trips, clapping during songs.

- Todd can be found: Winning at miniature golf, playing the violin, wetting the bed.

- Favorite snacks: Nachos "Flanders-style" (cucumbers with cottage cheese), wintergreen ice milk.

- Favorite games: Billy Graham's "Bible Blaster" video game (where players convert the heathens by firing Bibles at them); Good Samaritan, a board game (where players get to clothe the lepers and, instead of using dice, pieces are moved one space at a time because "it's less fun that way!").

- TV setup: Satellite (with over 230 channels locked out).

- Bedtime: Before sunset.

- Todd fact: His proudest possession is his Joseph of Arimathea trading card. ("26 conversions in A.D. 46!")

- Rod fact: He's jealous of girls, because they get to wear dresses.

Ned's List of Laudable Lefties

Ringo Starr • Herbert Hoover • Albert Einstein • Drew Barrymore • Linus Pauling • Friedrich Nietzsche • Keanu Reeves • Greta Garbo • Prince Charles • David Duchovny • Sandy Koufax • Edward R. Murrow • Oscar de la Hoya • Robert Redford • Ted Koppel • Jon Stewart • Winston Churchill • John F. Kennedy, Jr. • Caroline Kennedy • Peter Lawford • Prince William • Bill Mauldin • Ted Williams • Ben Hogan • Lenny Bruce • Bill Gates • Uri Geller • Mel Ott • 50 Cent • Mahatma Gandhi • Pablo Picasso • Richard Simmons • General H. Norman Schwarzkopf • Travis Barker • Johann Wolfgang von Goethe • Clarence Darrow • Milton Caniff • Bart Simpson • Fernando Valenzuela • Pat Robertson • John Dillinger • "Gentleman Jim" Corbett • Robert Crumb • Billy Corgan • Julia Roberts • Otto von Bismarck • Lewis Carroll • Pretty much any ballplayer named "Lefty" • Warren Spahn • Kurt Vonnegut • Ben Stiller • Leo Tolstoy • Babe Ruth • Colin Powell • Sergei Rachmaninoff • Al Gore • Paul Simon • Ricky Martin • H. G. Wells • Spike Lee • Eudora Welty • Eminem • Buzz Aldrin • Dick Dale • Fidel Castro • Henry Ford • Kermit the Frog • Albrecht Dürer • Deion Sanders • Bob Dylan • George S. Patton • The Everly Brothers • Judy Garland • Wally Joyner • Jimi Hendrix • Peter Fonda • David Robinson • Paul McCartney • Wolfgang Amadeus Mozart • Joey Heatherton • Matt Groening • Robert Plant • Cole Porter • Pelé • Dr. Albert Schweitzer • Seal • Joanne Woodward • M. C. Escher • Bill Russell • Sting • Rudy Vallee • Queen Victoria • Joe Perry • Michelangelo • Tom Cruise • Trey Parker • George Michael • Harry S Truman • Albert DeSalvo, The Boston Strangler • Raphael • Mark Spitz • Leonardo da Vinci • Oprah Winfrey • Fred Astaire • Johnny Rotten • Henri de Toulouse Lautrec • Marcia Clark • Robert Blake • Matthew Broderick • John McEnroe • Pierce Brosnan • Charlemagne • Hugh Jackman • Bobby Fischer • Ivan Lendl • Brett Butler • Carol Burnett • Ken Stabler • Pat Oliphant • George Burns • Isaac Hayes • Jake Gyllenhaal • Barry Bonds • Jason Bateman • Helen Keller • Jim Carrey • Ryan O'Neal • Ronald Reagan • Kurt Cobain • Whitey Ford • F. Lee Bailey • James Baldwin • Marshall McLuhan • Gayle Sayers • David Byrne • Oliver North • Dorothy Hamill • Charlie Chaplin • Angelina Jolie • Hans Conried • Maurice Ravel • Robert De Niro • Julius Caesar • W. C. Fields • H. Ross Perot • Cary Grant • Tippi Hedren • Jim Henson • Mark Brunell • Rock Hudson • Rod Laver • Jimmy Connors • Steve McQueen • Emma Thompson • Danny Kaye • Paul Klee • Diane Keaton • Larry Bird • Nicole Kidman • Harpo Marx • George H. W. Bush • Darryl Strawberry • Hans Holbein • Anne Meara • Marilyn Monroe • Ty Cobb • Kim Novak • David Letterman • Anthony Perkins • Rocky Balboa • Luke Perry • Robert McNamara • Ken Griffey Jr. • Richard Pryor • Eva Marie Saint • Jerry Seinfeld • "Shoeless" Joe Jackson • The Manhattan Transfer • Bruce Willis • Monica Seles • Rip Torn • Jim Zorn • Peter Ustinov • Dick Van Dyke • Steve Howe • Bill Clinton • William Windom • Bobby Orr • Bill Walton • James Cromwell • Calbert Cheaney • Tom Barrasso • Arnold Palmer • Martina Navratilova • Steve Forbes • Peter Jennings • Olivia de Havilland • Gerald Ford • Tim Allen • Matt Dillon • Lisa Kudrow • Cloris Leachman • Shirley MacLaine • Reggie Jackson • Kristy McNichol • J. Edgar Hoover • Marcel Marceau • Douglas Adams • Justice Ruth Bader Ginsberg • Carl Hubbell • Sarah Jessica Parker • Greg Louganis • Jay Leno • Lord Baden-Powell • Ripsa Koskinen-Papunen • Ehud • Whoopi Goldberg • Benjamin Franklin

THE SHARPEN'EDGE

Premium Selections from the Leftorium Catalog

From the Flancrest® line of high-end gadgets and doodily-doohickeys that no one needs but by gosh and by golly a fella's just gotta have!

Just-a-Half-a-Cup-More Left-handed Coffee Brewer

If you're like me, no matter how much java you have-a, you still want just a skosh more. Well, say no more, or should I say: say more! The Flancrest® Brewster serves up that perfect left-handed half-a-cup-a-coffee you crave. Its compact design lets it snuggle up on your kitchen counter in between your Flancrest® Brewhaha 12-cup left-handed coffeemaker and your Flancrest® Breuropean left-handed coffee espresso machine.

$129.99

Say "Y'ello-dily-odily!" to Our Left-handed Cell Phone

If you're like me, you miss a lot of important calls using a right-handed phone because you always have the wrong side up to your ear. That's why I think you'll flip over this flip phone with its exclusive left-handed keypad and a whole kit and caboodle of features so advanced you'll probably never learn to use 'em!

$59.99

Superbo Turbo-Thwacker Left-handed Weed Whacker

If you're like me, you know that no good weed goes unpunished. And nobody knows
punishment like the employees at the Thwacker Whacker factory. Their Turbo-
Thwacker transforms weed whackin' from a right-handed bore of a chore into
a left-handed ton o' fun! And the Thwacker's new turbocharger engine
now delivers increased noise levels up to 50%!

$49.99

Stylin' Left-handed Shoulder-Mount MP3 Tune Tote

If you're like me, you can never find your MP3 player because the li'l puppy is so gosh darn itsy
bitsy small. That's why I call this ultimate left-handed MP3 player accessory "The Big Woofer"!
Just slip your teensy-weensy MP3 player into the cradle and you're ready to tote dem tunes all
over town. Super-duper-size speakers eliminate the need
for those pesky earbuds.

$199.99

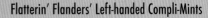

Flatterin' Flanders' Left-handed Compli-Mints

If you're like me, you know that nothing falls flatter than false flattery. That's why our Left-handed Compli-Mints take the "phony" out of "baloney." Box of 24 sweet-talkin' mints.

$3.99

Left-handed Nose Hair Styler

If you're like me, fellas, you know that the left hand "nose" best! And Ned "nose" you'll love this thingamabob that detangles, straightens, and adds body, giving you silky, shiny salon-styled nose hair—at home!

$29.99

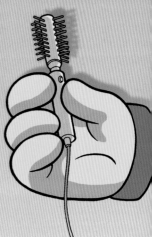

Tippity-top-tippin' Left-handed Hats

If you're like me, fellas, you like to tip your hat howdily-doodily-do when you meet a lady...but that's easier said than done when you're fumblin' to find the brim of a right-handed hat. Our nifteroonie left-handed hats will put you gents back in goodily graces with your gal pals quicker than you can say, "H-h-hats all, folks!"

$19.99

The Ned Flanders Signature Left-handed Pullover Sweater

"When Judgment Day comes, this is the sweater you'll reach for!" – Ned Flanders

If you're like me, you'll love this classic pullover sweater that harkens back to the days when us fellas didn't give a rooty-toot-toot about fashion. Men's sizes: Medium. Extra Medium. Extra Extra Medium. Available in green only.

$39.99

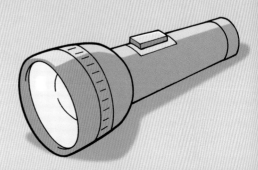

Left-handed Artists' Sofa-size Art Prints

If you're like me, you believe art should be a picture of something, not like that godless abstract stuff. That's why all of our sofa-size prints by left-handed artists depict actual, recognizable objects. Choose from such eye-pleasin' categories as: Plants & Flowers, Trees & Shrubs, Cows & Horses, Kittens & Puppies, and many, many more!

$99.99

"Let There Be Light!" Left-handed Flashlight

If you're like me, you hate to be in the dark when it comes to choosing a flashlight. Well then, let ol' Flash Flanders light up your life with this shining example! Our left-handed flashlight is so well designed you'll think it was designed by an intelligent designer.

$39.99

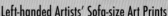

The MANY MANLY

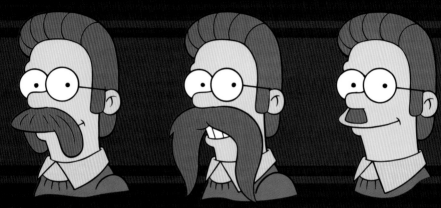

It Takes a Village, People!   I Am the Walrus—Goo Goo G'joob   Der Weiner Führer

Fu Man Choo-Choo   Hot Diggity Dog Diggity   Baron von Flanders

MUSTACHES *of* MAN

Whoopsie-Doodle

Ye Olde Mutton Chopster

Will o' the Wisp

Pencil Me In!

The Evil Diddily Doer

Well, Bust My Duster!

Anatomy of Ned

1. THE DIPPITY 'DO Just a little long on the sides and back, expressing the open-minded, anything-goes attitude you'd find at an all-day worship service featuring folk guitar! **2. FOUR EYES** Ned likes to keep his eyeglasses prescription just a wee tad off, because the world is so full of things no decent person should see! **3. THE OL' SOUP STRAINER** a.k.a. "The Nose Neighbor," "The Pushbroom," "The Cookie Duster," and "The Tickler" — Neddy's fabulous furry "freak flag" says he's not just another left-handed, self-employed, born-again conformist! **4. THE DEVIL'S DOORS** From rock music to cussing, more sin enters us through the ears than any other hole! That's why it's best to talk all you can and leave the listening to others! **5. THE SUPPER-SLURPIN' HYMN-HUMMER** Where the curly fries go in and the kumbayas come out! **6. PAINS IN THE NECK** Homer, Satan, the Post Office, and left-handed people who buy right-handed products! **7. CLOAK OF MODESTY** Covers the rock-cut abs and pecs Ned gets from "The Three Cs": Clean living, Chewing thoroughly, and a daily dose of vitamin Church! **8. SOUTHPAW** Ned's strong hand, and the inspiration for his professional passion: peddling pens, potato peelers, and patio polishers for the left-handed! **9. DON'T LOOK THERE! 10. PRAYIN' PERCHES** Catchers move to first base when the ol' knees give out, but Ned has no choice but to keep on kneelin'! Ouch! **11. RHYTHM STILTS** For cuttin' a rug in such community musical theater productions as "Oh! Streetcar!," "Long Day's Journey into Dance," "Glengarry Glen Jazz," "Tap on a Hot Tin Roof," and "Dreamgirls — and a Boy!" **12. PLAIN, COMFY SHOES** For walking away from trouble!

Situational Ethics or Traditional Moral Values?
My Way or the Higher Way? Confused? Just ask yourself:

WHAT WOULD NED DO?

"And God said, 'Take now thy son...and offer him there for a burnt offering upon one of the mountains...'"
— Genesis 22:2

Before you harmonize, don't just sanitize – Flanderize!

IT'S A REAL DILLY OF A PICKLE WHEN A FELLA CAN'T SING ALONG TO A SONG ON THE RADIO WITHOUT BLUSHING MORE SHADES OF RED THAN THE LIPSTICK RACK AT HAILSTONE'S FINE COSMETICS DEPARTMENT! THAT'S WHY BEFORE I CROON A TUNE, I LIKE TO GIVE THOSE GRIMY RHYMES A GOOD OL' FLANDERIZING!

SAFE LIKE ME

Don't cha wish your boyfriend was safe like me?
Don't cha wish your boyfriend was a wuss like me?
Don't cha? Don't cha?
Don't cha wish your boyfriend was tame like me?
Don't cha wish your boyfriend was dull like me?
Don't cha? Don't cha?
I know I'm rated G. I know we both agree.
I'm moderate, I'm meek and I'm mild.
I ain't lying. Look at me, I ain't wild.

Smells Like Teen Flanders

Hi-dilly-ho, hi-dilly-ho, hi-dilly-ho,
Hi-dilly-ho, hi-dilly-ho, hi-dilly-ho.
With the lights on it's less frightenin'.
Here we are now, Infotain us.
It's so safe yet enlightenin'.
Here we are now, Infotain us.
Okily-dokily, Indeedily-doodily,
Roger dodger, Super duper.
Yeah.

Scrub-a-Dub Flanders' Naughty Lyrics Laundry

BABY GOT TAX'D

I LIKE FLAT TAX AND I CANNOT LIE.
YOU OTHER VOTERS CAN'T DENY
THAT WHEN THE TAXMAN COMES WITH A TEN-FORTY FORM
ITEMIZED DEDUCTIONS ALL OVER THE PLACE,
YOU GET IRKED, WANNA PULL OUT YOUR HAIR
'CUZ YOU WISH THAT TAX WAS FLAT.
SO, VOTERS! (YEAH!) VOTERS! (YEAH!)
HAS YOUR BABY GOT FLAT TAX? (HECK YEAH!)
TELL 'EM TO FLATTEN IT! (FLAT TAX!) FLAT TAX! (FLAT TAX!)
FLATTEN THAT INCOME TAX!
BABY GOT TAX'D...BABY GOT TAX'D.

It's Hard Out Here for a Ned

You know it's hard out here for a Ned.
When he livin' on a right-handed planet
With a left-handed man taken for granted,
Because a whole lot of righties outta spite
Will have a whole lot of lefties
writing right.

JESUS FREAK

OHHHHH.
JESUS FREAK, JESUS FREAK.
THAT GIRL'S A JESUS FREAK.
OHHHHH.
SHE'S A VERY GODLY GIRL,
THE KIND YOU TAKE HOME
TO YOUR MOTHER.
SHE WILL NEVER LET OL' JESUS DOWN
ONCE SHE SEES HIM ON THE CROSS.
OW, GIRL!

A NED FLANDERS' COOKBOOK!

AUTHENTICO CHIPS AND FIERY SALSA

Take a trip south of the border without all the scary peppers and fryin' oil! You won't know whether to say grace or "gracias!"

- 1 package of Krusty's Saltine-esque White Crackers™
- 1 bottle of catsup (any brand that spells it that way)
- 1 teaspoon of pepper

Pour catsup in bowl, mix in pepper. Break crackers into chip-like triangles. Serve in a colorful (but not too colorful) dip bowl and plate.

CHICKEN CURRY

My friend Apu got me curious about Indian food; then, after walking into an Indian restaurant and smellin' the cuisine, I got less curious. Still, I thought I'd give it a whirl the Flanders way.

4 chicken bosoms • 2 tsp. salt • 1 jar yellow mustard • 1 head iceberg lettuce

Boil the chicken for one to two hours. Place boiled chicken atop lettuce leaves on a platter. Sprinkle with salt and serve with a side of mustard for dippin'.

Ol' Time Chicago Hot Dog

Enjoy the idea of eating a Chicago hot dog but unsure about the influence of a big, morally bankrupt city? Try my wholesome take on the tube steak!

• 1 carrot • 1 large celery stalk • 1 can of Krusty Kanned Cheese Product™

Place carrot in celery stalk, putting a mustardlike squiggle of cheese on the carrot. Eat while pretending it's a hot dog.

Falafel

Here's an all-American take on a Middle Eastern staple, with all the crunch and none of the excitement.

1 cup of plain croutons • 1 hot dog bun
•1 tsp. of ranch dressing

Toast hot dog bun. Fill toasted bun with croutons. Pour ranch dressing over croutons and serve.

DEVIL'S FOOD CAKE

Sure, you've saved room for dessert, but sometimes, it's the dessert that needs savin'!

• 1 package of devil's food cake mix
• 1 quart of holy water

Prepare mix according to package. Bring in a priest or pastor to exorcise the cake with holy water. Pray seven minutes for the cake, followed by the singing of a hymn. Cut into pieces and serve directly from the pan, using leftover holy water for dippin'.

ASK-AROONIE the NEDSTER!

HEY-DILLY-HO, KIDIDDLES. SO WHO'S GOT A **Q** IN NEED OF AN **A**?

WHAT'S THE MEANING OF LIFE?

I EAT CORN.

WHY DID THE CHICKEN CROSS THE ROAD?

I MEAN, WHO'S GOT A **Q** ABOUT THE **BIBLE**!

HOW DO WE KNOW THAT EVERYTHING IN THE BIBLE IS TRUE?

BECAUSE GOD **HIMSELF SPOKE** THESE WORDS AND THE FORTY OR SO FELLAS WHO WROTE THE BIBLE THEN COPIED THEM DOWN. NATURA-DIDDLY, WHEN I SAY "**COPIED**" I AM SPEAK-ING IN THE **BIBLICAL** SENSE, NOT THE **XEROXICAL** SENSE.

HOW DO WE KNOW THE WRITERS **REALLY** WROTE THE **WORD OF GOD** AND DIDN'T JUST MAKE UP A BUNCH OF STUFF?

INDEEDILY-DOODILY, MISS DOUBTING THOMASINA. IT IS A MIGHTY BIG-DIGGILY CLAIM TO MAKE, BUT IT'S **TRUE**! IF IT WERE FALSE, THEN THE FELLAS WHO WROTE THE SCRIPTURES WOULD HAVE BEEN LYING, OR INSANE, OR BOTH.

SO IS THIS A **TRUE/FALSE** QUESTION OR MULTIPLE CHOICE?

Ned Answers Kids' Questions About Religion

NED'S LIFETIME TO-DIDDLY-DIDDLY-DO LIST!

- Spend a weekend at Dollywood.
- Make my own mayonnaise.
- Surf the Sea of Galilee.
- Train for and ultimately try hot sauce.
- Knit my own sweater.
- Learn Aramaic.
- Swim with a dolphin and attempt to convert it.
- Wear flip-flops.
- Try butter on my popcorn.
- Fish.
- See all of Don Knotts' films.
- Enter the Pro Bumper Pool circuit.
- Bowl a "double perfect" game — one right-handed, one left-handed.
- "Hot tub-it" in apple cider.
- Mustache-wise, go for the full handlebar.

- Visit Branson, Missouri.
- Have one of my jokes bought by "Reader's Digest."
- Invent a softer, crust-free white bread.
- Win a chili cook-off.
- Recover over 80% of the items I loaned to Homer.
- Create a flavor between "vanilla" and "plain."
- Make it to the finish line without a single cavity.
- Build a house for someone.
- Spend a summer with Rod and Todd, driving around to the great cathedrals of the United States.
- Win the National Praying Bee.
- See what all the fuss is about tomatoes.
- Complete my secret "Snork" collection.
- Translate the Bible into Pig Latin.
- Create the ultimate "alternative to swearing" word.
- Anoint the sores on the feet of the poor in every state of the Union.
- Meet Tom Wilson, the creator of "Ziggy."
- Attend a taping of "America's Funniest Home Videos."
- Go all the way with it and get ordained.
- Try to achieve a negative carbon footprint.
- Make up for bragging that one time about being humble.
- Trademark "diddly."
- Give sunglasses a whirl.
- Gently help Homer realize the horrific error of his ways.

JUNIOR CAMPER'S OATH

I hereby swear (as an oath and not as a cuss word)
That neither rain, nor sleet, nor gobs of crud
Hurled at me by schoolyard thugs,
Nor snow, nor slush, nor gloom of despair
Brought on by my rejection by
the popular crowd,
Nor haze, nor hail, nor the
pitying stares of pretty girls,
Nor drought, nor drizzle, nor
temptation in the form of an
all-syrup, Super-Size Squishee,
Nor heat, nor humidity,
nor an itchy rash in my underpants,
Nor the voices in my head,
Nor fog, nor smog, nor cyclonic winds
between 30 and 64 knots,
Nor being called a weenie, a wimp,
a wuss, or worse,
Shall keep me from doing
my darndest
To do my duty to God
and to Springfield.

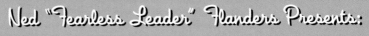
Ned "Fearless Leader" Flanders Presents:

JUNIOR CAMPER MERIT BADGES EARNED IN RECOGNITION OF MERITORIOUS ACHIEVEMENT

BEHAVING NICELY

LO-CARB, NONFAT COOKOUT JAMBOREE

PARTY POOPING

EARLY TAX FILING

PUSSYFOOTING

FUTURE REPUBLICAN CONGRESSMAN

BUTTER KNIFE SAFETY

WON'T ASK WON'T TELL

FATHER/SON RAFTING TRIP SURVIVOR

GOD PLEASING

BURNING MARSHMALLOWS FIRE PATROL

BIBLE THUMPING

BUZZ KILLING

FLAG WAVING

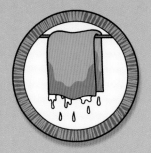

WET BLANKETRY

MILDLIFE MANAGEMENT

TEETOTALING

FIRST-CLASS WUSS

FUDDY DUDDY BUDDY

PACK MENTALITY

BED-WETTING

FUSSBUDGETING

LEGAL PARKING

GOD THE ALPHA AND THE OMEGA, MAKER OF HEAVEN AND EARTH

God is the creator of the universe and the source of our knowledge of right and wrong. Ned maintains a very close relationship with Him, communicating His desires to anyone who will listen and asking Him favors on a minute-by-minute basis. That close bond was tested when the Almighty One allowed the Flanders' home to be destroyed in a hurricane; however, after a brief course of psychotherapy, Ned forgot he had ever had a problem with God.

- Quote: "Okily-dokily, Ned!"

- Typically miraculous accomplishment: Created Ned.

- What keeps Him from being too good to be true: Works in mysterious ways (created Homer Simpson).

- Most comforting trait: Knows how many hairs are in Ned's mustache.

- Loves: Everyone (even Homer Simpson), but watch out for his temper.

- Height: Infinite.

- Weight: So big He can't lift himself—or can He?

- Skills: All of them.

- Faults: None.

- Turn-ons: Obedience, hymns, church, the Springfield Isotopes, the USA, Ned's religion.

- Turn-offs: Sin, popular music, Hollywood, evolution, the Shelbyville Visitors, other countries, other religions.

The Devil is Prince of Darkness and ruler of Hell, a place of eternal punishment where people like Homer Simpson go when they die. He likes the place full, so he tempts people into committing punishable sins (such as borrowing tools from Ned and never returning them) and tries to get them to sign their souls over to him in exchange for favors (such as donuts).

- Quote: "You Americans with your 'due process' and 'fair trials'! This is always so much easier in Mexico!"

- Physical characteristics: Goat legs, horns, many faces (but he has been known to look like Ned because "It's always the one you least suspect!")

- Associates: Benedict Arnold, Lizzie Borden, Richard Nixon, John Wilkes Booth, Blackbeard the Pirate, John Dillinger, and the starting line of the 1976 Philadelphia Flyers.

- Acquaintances: Bart Simpson, Mr. Burns.

- Enemies: God, Ned Flanders.

- Turn-ons: Ironic punishments, legal documents, trials, trials by fire, fire, heavy metal music.

- Turn-offs: "Parental Warning" stickers, fair trials, angry Amish farmers with pitchforks, when Bart teases him by offering to sell him his soul and then changes his mind.

NEDDY NO-NO'S
Words Forbidden in the Flanders Home

A COMIC BOOK OF VIRTUES

GOING OUT FOR A QUICK JIGGITY-JOG, BOYS. GOTTA KEEP THE OL' SHIP IN SHAPE!

BUT ISN'T THAT *VANITY*, DADDY? AND ISN'T VANITY *A SIN*?

"FORGIVE US THIS DAILY JOG, FOR WE SWEAT UNTO OUR GARMENTS AS ONE WHO IS UNCLEAN, AND ALL OUR RIGHTEOUSNESS BREAKETH LIKE THE WIND." **JASON 9:18**

WELL, NOW...

AND DOES NOT ADVERBS 6:16 TELL US THAT THE LORD *DETESTETH* VANITY?

"THERE ART SEVEN THINGS THE LORD HATETH— AND VANITY, ALTHOUGH IT COMETH IN AT NUMBER EIGHT, IS NONETHELESS AN ABOMINATION TO HIM." **ADVERBS 6:16**

WELL, OKILY-DOKILY, THEN I'LL HUSTLE MY BUSTLE INTO THE KITCHEN AND RUSTLE US UP SOME SCRUM-DIDDILY-UMPTIOUS VITTLES!

BUT, DADDY, THAT'S *GLUTTONY*, AND IF WE COMMIT THE SIN OF GLUTTONY, WE WON'T GET TO GO SEE MOMMY UP IN HEAVEN!

"IT IS EASIER FOR A 'C' STUDENT TO GET INTO YALE THAN FOR AN OBESE MAN TO ENTER THE KINGDOM OF HEAVEN." **PHILIPIPHLOPPIANS 4:8**

WHAT ARE YOU DOING, DADDY?

OH, JUST TRIMMIN' THE OL' COOKIE DUSTER.

BUT, DADDY, I READ IN LEVIS 5:01 THAT "YE SHALT NOT TRIM THY BEARD."

WELL SURE, BUT THAT'S THE *OLD TESTAMENT*, YOU SEE, AND NOWADAYS A MAN HAS TO KEEP UP HIS APPEARANCES...

"YE SHALL CUT NOT THY BEARD; NOR SHALL YE SHAVE THY LEGS; NOR WAX THY PALMS OR KNUCKLES." **LEVIS 5:01**

BUT THAT'S *PRIDE*, DADDY! THE LORD DEEMS PRIDE TO BE *WICKED*!

"PRIDE GOETH BEFORE PREJUDICE, AND I BEFORE YE EXCEPT AFTER THEE." **ISAYSO 16:18**

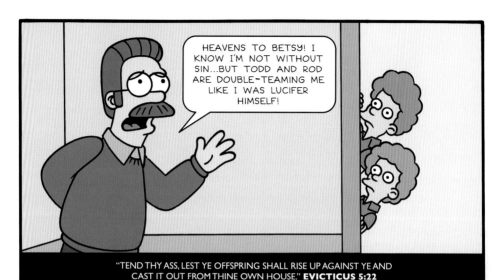

"TEND THY ASS, LEST YE OFFSPRING SHALL RISE UP AGAINST YE AND CAST IT OUT FROM THINE OWN HOUSE." **EVICTICUS 5:22**

"THUS WAS SAID TO PETER, PAUL, AND MARY: 'TAKETH THE BLASPHEMER AND LET YE STONE HIM UNTO DEATH, AND LET HE WHO PITCHED LAST SEASON'S SHUTOUT GAME CAST THE FIRST STONE.'" **HEY JUDE 24:16**

SHOW ME THE EXIT, O LORD

KIDS' END TIMES FUN ZONE

1. Four Horsemen of the Apocalypse Merry-Go-Round
2. Leviticus 26:22 House of Horrors
3. Rapture – The Ride
4. Numbered Beasts Petting Zoo

FEAR O' GOD SPINE-TINGLY-DINGLING THRILL RIDES

5. Holy Roller Coaster
6. Step Out in Faith Freefall
7. King David's Wild Ride

MORE HOLIER THAN THOU-SAND ISLANDS

8. Jumpin' Jesus Freaks Jamboree
9. It's a Cruel World Pavilion
10. God-Forbid-You-Should-Put-Your-Eye-Out Shooting Gallery

ARMAGEDDON OUTTA HERE!

11. Satan's Tunnel of Lust
12. The Lord's Wrath Highway to Hell
13. Tiny Tots Ferris Wheel of Sin

SHOPS & RESTAURANTS

14. Immaculate Conceptions Gift Boutique
15. Bible Belts & Hats
16. Goody Two-Shoes & Socks
17. Forbidden Fruit Stand
18. Knee-Benders
19. The Last Supper Café
20. Pillar o' Salt Fish 'n' Chips
21. Adam's BBQ Ribs
22. Reverend Lovejoy's Cruci-Fixin's

ACCOMMODATIONS

23. Ye Olde No Room at the Inn Resort
24. Mahmoud and Yun Hee's Tower of Babel B 'n' B
25. A Child Left Behind Day Care

PRAISELAND SOUVENIR MAP

They Shot Bambi's Mom!

At the Circus

Li'l League Loser

Lost at the Mall

Daddy's New Lady Friend

Mother's Little Helper

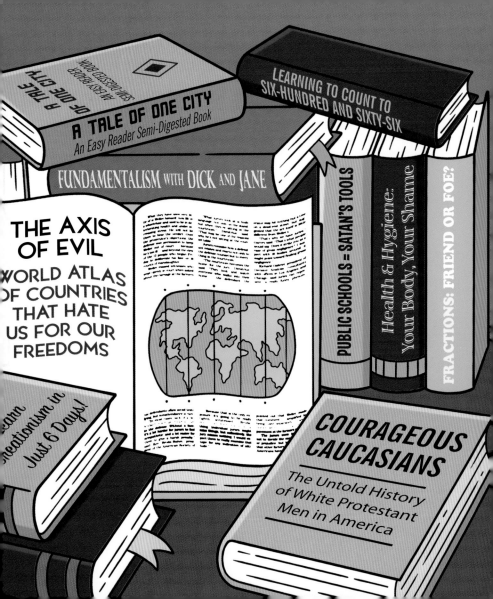

ASK-AROONIE the NEDSTER!

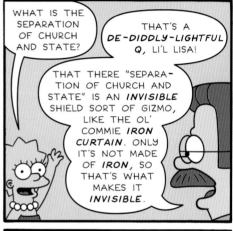

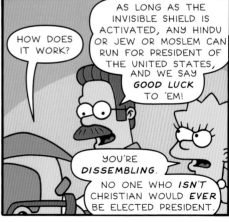

Ned Answers Kids' Questions About Religion

THAT'S BECAUSE *CHRISTIANITY* IS AMERICA'S *BRAND-NAME RELIGION!* WHAT SAYS *"AMERI-CAN-DO"* BETTER THAN OUR GOOD OL' BLUE-EYED, BLOND-HAIRED *JESUS* WITH HIS BUMPER STICKERS AND TRUCKER HATS AND T-SHIRTS AND COFFEE MUGS AND TOTE BAGS AND REFRIGERATOR MAGNETS?

COOL! I'M GOING TO GET A *JESUS* TATTOO ON MY BUTT!

DON'T YOU THINK IT'S CRASS CONSUMERISM TO REDUCE JESUS TO A LICENSING AND MERCHANDISING TRADEMARK, NOT TO MENTION A DECORATION FOR BART'S BUTT?

GOODILY HEAVENS *NO!* THE $3 BILLION A YEAR RELIGIOUS GIFT INDUSTRY IS A REAL WING DINGER OF A WITNESSING TOOL!

A WELL-PLACED BUMPER STICKER CAN BRING A REAR-ENDER TO CHRIST.

OH. MY. GOD.

FLANDERS APPROVED
OKILY-DOKILY LYRICS

NED'S NIX and PICKS FROM THE

"Approved" is a notice that Ned has deemed the recording to be
tame, tepid, and completely unremarkable.

"NED'S PICKS" TOP SIX

Whitney Dallas–Fort Worth
The Most Greatest God-Blessed Song
of All (1986)
✔✔✔✔ Ned said: "De-diddily-lightful!"

U Too?
Oh, For Chrissake (1992)
✔✔✔ Ned said: "Fan-diddily-tastic!"

Negroes Without Attitudes
Straight on up to Middle Management
(1989)
✔✔ Ned said: "Up-diddily-lifting!"

The Super-Duper Amazing Jesus Freak
Express Soundtrack (1969)
✔✔✔✔ Ned said: "Hi ho-diddily-
wholesome fun!"

White Bread
Hold the Mayo (1976)
✔✔ Ned said: "Toe-diddily-tappingly
irresistible!"

Billy Joe Bobby Leroy, Jr.
Yee-haw, America! (2002)
✔✔✔ Ned said: "Gosh-diddily darn swell!"

FLAP DOODLE* MUSIC ALBUM ARCHIVES

"Advisory" is a notice to concerned parents that a recording contains coarse language and/or references to s_x outside the confines of marriage to such an extent that Ned freaked out when he heard it.

"NED'S NIX" TOP SIX

Lukewarm Cranberry Pumpkins
D.O.A.! at the Springfield Coliseum
(1997)
✓✓ Ned said: "Eek!"

The Boogie Machine
Dirty Filthy Disco Dancing (1978)
✓✓✓ Ned said: "Yikes!"

Mad Donna
Like So Totally NOT a Virgin. Duh.
(1986)
✓✓✓✓ Ned said: "Tsk. Tsk."

Sgt. Psychedelic's Flower-Powered
Free Love Band
High As a Kite (1967)
✓✓✓ Ned said: "Nay!"

The Bachelors Four
Songs for Swingin' Singles (1962)
✓✓ Ned said: "Oh, dear!"

Boy Band 2 Menz & Back
Skanky As She Wanna B (2001)
✓✓✓✓✓ Ned said: "What?"

*Flanders Lyrics Advisory Program: Designated Obscene or Okily-Dokily for Little Ears

REVEREND TIMOTHY LOVEJOY SPIRITUAL LEADER OF SPRINGFIELD

Sometimes zealous, sometimes positively mellow, Reverend Lovejoy is a clergyman of contradiction. As the poorly paid spiritual leader of the Springfield Community Church, he tries to instill morality into the townsfolk, with mixed results. At one end of the spectrum, he tries to gently move Homer Simpson towards the church—at the other, he tries to gently move Ned Flanders away from it. Whether he wants to be or not, Lovejoy is often at the center of Springfield's greatest controversies, or at the very least, he comments on them in his weekly sermon. And though he has called for the burning of books and clown-related merchandise, he has also been known to swear and attend dinner theater. Ultimately, Reverend Lovejoy seems his happiest alone in his basement, playing with his model railroad and wearing a conductor's hat.

● Quote: "And as we pass the collection plate, please give as though the person next to you were watching."

● Tone: Mono.

● Secret ambition: To entertain the world with stirring acoustic guitar renditions of "The Entertainer" and "Michael, Row the Boat Ashore."

● Other jobs: Regular panelist on "Gabbin' About God" on KBBL radio, leads services at Springfield Prison, drives the Springfield Book-burning Mobile.

● Hobbies: Model trains, starting or joining angry mobs, bowling.

● Signs that he doesn't earn much: He has to fix the church organ himself, he perpetually borrows his Bible from the library, he once had to wear an ad for Fatso's Hash House on his robe to help pay for church repairs, the Kwik-E-Mart will not accept his checks.

● How Kent Brockman describes him: "Local Bible Nut."

● Description of the world's religious makeup: Christian, Jew, miscellaneous.

● On the Bible: "You ever sit down and read this thing? Technically, we're not allowed to go to the bathroom."

Helen Lovejoy, wife of Reverend Lovejoy and mother of Jessica, is one of the most prominent voices of morality in Springfield—both calling for said morality and telling tales of its violation through her constant gossiping. Regarding gossip, she prefers homegrown, small-town scandal to tabloid headlines. In the past, she vowed to use her gossip for good, though there is no record of her actually doing so.

- Quote: "Won't somebody please think of the children?"

- Hates: Michelangelo's David, losing, being out of the loop, alcohol.

- Loves: Gossip, judging others, bowling, dining out, testifying against people, twisting the knife, piling on.

- Secret shame: Allegedly dyes her hair.

- Affiliations: The Investorettes, the Holy Rollers, S.N.U.H. (Springfieldians for Nonviolence, Understanding, and Helping).

- Acting credits: Stella, in a Springfield Community Theater Production of "Oh! Streetcar!"

- Favorite magazine: "Parade."

- Her chosen adjective to describe the Middle East conflict: Iffy.

- Her perfect Sunday: A hearty breakfast, church, hearing about/seeing something scandalous in town, spending the afternoon on the phone telling a dozen people, some tennis, dinner at Luigi's with her husband.

40 TYPES OF PEOPLE

THE CATNAPPER

THE RESTLESS
TOE TAPPER

THE JITTERY
NICOTINE FIEND

THE HAPPY
HEAD NODDER

THE DRY COUGHER

THE GODLESS
GUM POPPER

THE WIDE-EYED
SNOOZER

THE HAREBRAINED
SNIGGLER

THE HYMN HUMMER

THE COLLECTION
PLATE KLEPTO

THE NONCHALANT
NOSE PICKER

THE HOLY TERROR

THE HEAVER OF
AUDIBLE SIGHS

THE DEADLY
GAS PASSER

THE FREE-THINKING
LOOSE CANNON

THE ELBOW NUDGER

THE CLOSE, PERSONAL
FRIEND OF GOD

THE BENCHWARMER

THE SMELLY
OLD COOT

THE VISION SEEKER

YOU MEET IN CHURCH

THE MOUTH
BREATHER

THE DERANGED
AMEN SHOUTER

THE GUILT-RIDDEN
THUMB TWIDDLER

THE GAPING YAWNER

THE BAWLING BABY

THE WHEEZING
GEEZER

THE SMUG
EYEBROW RAISER

THE PIGEON-HEARTED
SWOONER

THE INCOHERENT
PRAYER MUTTERER

THE CANDY WRAPPER
RUSTLER

THE DAMNED
IF YOU DO

THE DAMNED
IF YOU DON'T

THE CELL PHONE
YAKKER

THE SANCTIMONIOUS
BUSYBODY

THE WRISTWATCH
WATCHER

THE MALCONTENT
PEW POTATO

THE "JESUS LOVES
YOU, MAN!" MAN

THE STARER
INTO THE VOID

THE TRUE BELIEVER

THE BIBLE SNIFFER

I've been tryin' to help my neighboreeno-numero-uno Homer Simpson to get regular for years...about church! Yesterday, I loaned him my brand-new HD-DVD player with one li'l con-diddly-dition: he had to tell me what it'd take for him to get lurchin' towards churchin'. Well, just like when Martin Luther nailed those good ol' 95 Theses to the church door, Homer stuck this drawing to the hood of my car with some gum. Behold, friends...

HOMER SIMPSON'S DREAM CHURCH!

1. Holy Water Slide.
2. Baptism Wave Pool.
3. Retractable roof (for getting closer to God and post-service fireworks displays).
4. 24-Hour Pancake Breakfast/Dinner/Snack-a-teria.
5. Individual ejector seat pews for quick escapes.
6. Altar-adjacent omelet bar and carving station.
7. Movie theater (for screenings of uplifting, spiritual movies like "Oh, God!," "Thank God It's Friday," "The Exorcist," "Monty Python and the Holy Grail," "Wholly Moses!," "Bruce Almighty," and "Cannonball Run II").
8. GOD: THE RIDE! (with full-motion, gyroscope-enabled pews).
9. Livestock area dedicated to raising REAL animals for the Nativity scene (and the carving station).
10. Chicken coop (for farm-fresh Easter Eggs and altar-adjacent omelet bar).
11. Personal TVs built into the back of every pew (with all religious channels blocked out).
12. Bible humidor.
13. Leper colony/guest cottages for visiting clergy.
14. Leper viewing area.
15. Chili river.
16. Beer guy.
17. Worship band: U2.
18. Costumed church mascot: Howie, the Holy Mackerel.

That Ol' Dingily-ding Dang Church 'n' State Debate

THE 10 COMMANDMENTS

Thou shalt not take the name of the Lord thy God in vain.

Thou shalt not kill.

Thou shalt have no other gods before me.

Thou shalt not commit adultery.

Thou shalt not steal.

Thou shalt not bow down to false idols, nor serve them.

Thou shalt not covet thy neighbor's house, nor thy neighbor's wife, nor his ox...

Thou shalt honor thy father and thy mother.

Thou shalt not bear false witness against thy neighbor.

Remember the Sabbath Day, to keep it holy.

vs. THE BILL OF RIGHTS

You have freedom of speech.

You have the right to bear arms.

You have freedom from
other people's religion.

You have the right to remain silent.
And if you're in the military,
"Don't ask, don't tell."

You have the right to an attorney.

You have the right to burn a flag.
If you cannot afford a flag,
one will be provided for you.

Three strikes and you're out.

Legal control of a parent over a
child is terminated at age 18.

You have the right of access
to 24-hour cable news…

…and to upgrade to our 120-channel
Premium Sports Package!

NED-APPROVED
FAMILY-SAFE*
TV VIEWING LOG

*NOTE: Shows that start after 7:00 PM are for GROWNUPS ONLY!

SUNDAY

7:00 AM
(132) *BROTHER FAITH'S FAITH-OFF* (Faith-healing) — Brother Faith makes a lame man walk, a blind woman see, and a prayer partner's life savings disappear.

8:00 PM
(13) *THE SAMSONS* (Comedy) — Animated laughs and feats of strength from "that modern Old Testament family!"

8:30 PM
(13) *KING OF THE HILL* (Religion) — The Sermon on the Mount, directed by Mel Gibson. (Graphic violence.)

MONDAY

6:00 AM
(238) *SIT STILL* (Children) — Today let's see who can be the quietest.

5:00 PM
(132) *FAMILY BAYWATCH* (Drama) — Classic episodes digitally remastered with modest swimwear.

8:00 PM
(7) *FOUND* (Drama) — Plane crash survivors stranded on an island start a church congregation.

9:00 PM
(4) *HEROES* (Reality) — Real-life stories of ordinary citizens who monitor TV shows, music, and movies for objectionable content, then complain to the government.

TUESDAY

5:00 PM
(53) *COVER THEIR EYES!* (Horror) — Men in rubber monster costumes chase women in one-piece bathing suits, giving parents at home a family-bonding opportunity to cover their children's eyes.

5:30 PM
(99) *FUTURAMA* (Religion) — Two years in the future, the faithful are whisked into heaven while unbelievers are left behind to rot.

8:00 PM
(658) *ARRESTED DEVELOPMENT* (Education) — Tips on protecting your kids from outside influences. Tonight: avoiding "ladies' products" in the bathroom.

WEDNESDAY

5:00 PM
(52) *REVEREND WHO* (Creation Science Fiction) — The Reverend travels 5,000 years into the past to help early humans survive a dinosaur attack.

9:00 PM
(FOOD FOR THE SOUL NETWORK)
THE GOD-FEARING GOURMET (Cooking) — Stretch a fish sandwich to feed a crowd. Plus: secrets of turning water into wine.

THURSDAY

6:00 AM
(238) *IN OR OUT* (Children) — The kids learn to keep the screen door closed.

7:00 PM
(ETERNAL LIFETIME) *INTELLIGENT DESIGN* (Design) — Homeowners remodel their living spaces as the Creator intended.

8:00 PM
(FOX) *FALSE IDOL* (Reality) — Young singers who are too full of themselves get taken down a peg.

FRIDAY

6:00 PM
(13) *RADIO* (Drama) — Inspiring stories with no picture so you can use your imagination, not like today.

9:00 PM
(4) *DATELINE: POSTMARK* (News Magazine) — Investigative reporters expose abuses at the post office. Tonight: it's all "Rush, rush! Getcha in, getcha out!"

SATURDAY

6:00 AM
(238) *CLEAN YOUR PLATE* (Children) — Tofu stir-fry. (Repeat)

3:00 PM
(YARD) *AMERICA'S DOING YARDWORK!* (Infotainment) — Suburban husbands face satisfying outdoor challenges (Live).

9:00 PM
(110) *ZONING SQUAD* (Adventure) — A world-weary veteran and an idealistic rookie see to it that premises are put to proper use.

10:00 PM
(FOX) *SO YOU THINK YOU CAN PRAY* (Reality) — It's the ultimate search for the nation's best worshipper! After a nationwide casting call, the most faithful will take part in a grueling 12-week competition in which some will collapse under the pressure, others will reveal their two left hands, and one will pray his or her way into God's heart!

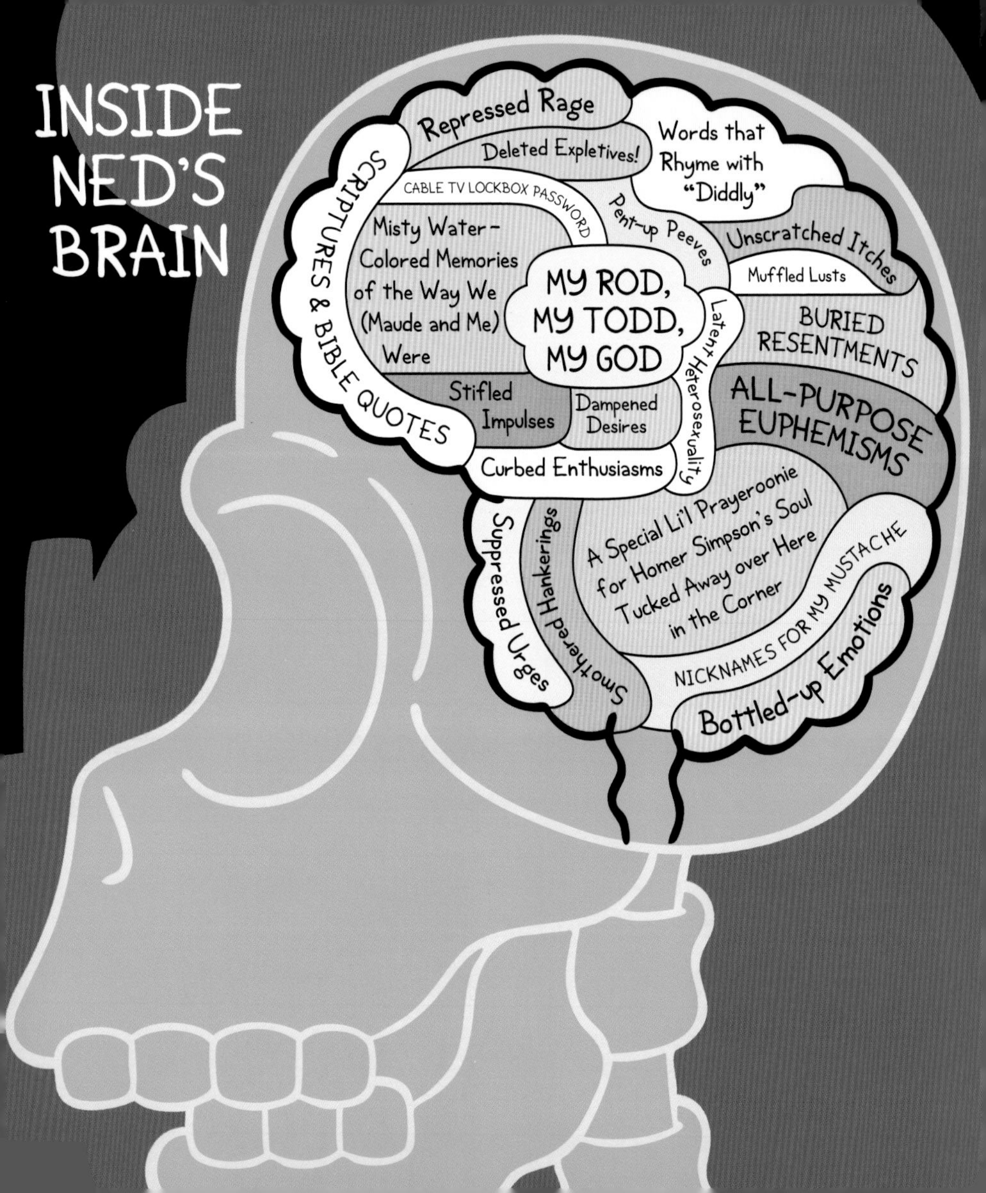

INSIDE NED'S BRAIN

Repressed Rage

Deleted Expletives!

Words that Rhyme with "Diddly"

SCRIPTURES & BIBLE QUOTES

CABLE TV LOCKBOX PASSWORD

Misty Water-Colored Memories of the Way We (Maude and Me) Were

Pent-up Peeves

Unscratched Itches

Muffled Lusts

MY ROD, MY TODD, MY GOD

BURIED RESENTMENTS

Latent Heterosexuality

ALL-PURPOSE EUPHEMISMS

Stifled Impulses

Dampened Desires

Curbed Enthusiasms

A Special Li'l Prayeroonie for Homer Simpson's Soul Tucked Away over Here in the Corner

Suppressed Urges

Smothered Hankerings

NICKNAMES FOR MY MUSTACHE

Bottled-up Emotions

Situational Ethics or Traditional Moral Values?
My Way or the Higher Way? Confused? Just ask yourself:
WHAT WOULD NED DO?

"If sinners entice thee, consent thou not."
— Proverbs 1:10

HEY THERE, WHEN THE GOOD FOLKS OF SPRINGFIELD THROW THE **DEVIL** A BIRTHDAY BASH, I **PRETEND** TO GO ALONG WITH IT! OTHERWISE, I'M JUST PUTTIN' THE **RUDE** IN **PRUDE**! BUT I DRAW THE LINE AT CAUSIN' MY WEE ONES ANY FREAKY FRIGHTMARES! NO REASON TO FRET THEIR FOGGY NOGGINS ABOUT GHOULIES 'N' GHOSTIES, AT LEAST 'TIL THEY'RE 21 **OR** MARRIED (WHICHEVER COMES LAST)! THAT'S WHY I MAKE SURE THEY'RE DOODLIN' DADDY'S THE ONE TO EXPLAIN ALL THE LORE AND LEGENDS BEHIND...

COUNT JUICEBOX

He vants to drink...his juice! And his chompers are just sharp enough to chomp open the box!

FRANKY THE CLOWN

Look at the size of them clodhoppers! And that funny green facepaint! And the goofy Beatle wig! And the silly doodads on his neck! Yep, he's a clown, all right! Sure is!

...ROD AND TODD-SAFE HALLOWEEN COSTUMES

TRIMMY McSKINNY

This dynamic dieter will skip the sugary treats, thank you very much! He'd rather munch on some healthy Trick-or-Beets!

MR. MUSTACHE

He likes growin' his cookie duster even more than Daddy does. So much so, he grew an all-over soup strainer! Nice fella, too!

LAZARUS

Lazarus moaned, "I've breathed my last!" The Good Lord chuckled, "Not so fast!" When there's faith in your heart, the night of the livin' dead's just a good-time jamboree!

BUCKY BEDSHEET

He keeps you cool when it's hot and cozy-ish when it's cold! And in case of an accident, just throw him in the washer! He likes the spin cycle best!

THE NICE OLD CLEANING LADY AT THE CHURCH

Actually, Rod made this one for himself.
Me, I like to see him dress a little more like a fella!

BANDAGE BUDDY

Boo-boos and owies better watch out!
He's trussin' the troubles of every
scamp with a scrape!

Deep within the bowels of the Flanderosa lies one of the greatest nonoffensive film collections ever assembled! Behold...

NED'S DVD SHELF!

SOME LIKE IT LUKEWARM TO MILDLY TEMPERATE

It's a Sane, Sane, Sane, Sane World

MY BIG, FAT SECOND BAPTISM

The Bad News Cross Bearers

Lord of the Rings and Everything Else

WILLARD SCOTT'S GREATEST BIRTHDAY WISHES

THE LION, THE WITCH, AND THE WARDROBE: THE OVERTLY RELIGIOUS CUT

BORN AGAIN ON THE FOURTH OF JULY

WALKING ON THE WATERFRONT

Abbott and Costello Meet Someone Really Nice

Tootsie (The Non–Cross Dressing Version)

12 CONTENTED MEN

ASK-AROONIE *the* NEDSTER!

Ned Answers Kids' Questions About Religion

WHAT SAY WE JUST *SKIP* THE *Q*'S AND *A*'S AND THE OL' NEDSTER WILL READ FROM THE FLANDERS' *FAMILY-FRIENDLY* BIBLE. THIS ONE'S A REAL *CORKER!* IT'S THE STORY OF THE FOUR HORSIES OF THE CATACLYSM: *BOILS, SCABS, SORES, AND PUS*.

"*LO AND BEHOLD!* A LOUD VOICE CAME FROM THE SKY SAYING, '*HOWDILY-DOODILY, SINNERS!* I GOT ONE *DILLY* OF A *WAKE-UP CALL COMIN' YOUR WAY!*' AND THUS WAS SENT DOWN UPON THE EARTH A *MUCHO BIGGO EARTHQUAKE,* AND A WHOLE BUNCH OF FOLKS WERE THROWN *ALIVE* INTO A SEA OF *BURNING ACID*. THEY *GNAWED* THEIR TONGUES AND *BLASPHEMED* GOD BECAUSE OF THE *PAIN*. AND THUS WAS VISITED UPON *THEIR CHILDREN* THE *FOUR HORSIES OF THE CATACLYSM* WHICH BROUGHT UPON THE TYKES A *PLAGUE* OF *ITCHY, SCRATCHY SCABS* THAT BECAME *GINORMOUS OOZING SORES*. THE LI'L KIDIDDLES TRIED TO SKEDADDLE, BUT WERE SOON CURSED WITH *EVIL BOILS* THAT COVERED THEIR FLESH IN *PUS-FILLED* ABUNDANCE FOR *SEVEN GENERATIONS!*"

GODSPEED, LITTLE DOODLES!

SLAM!

I *SPOILED* MYSELF.

WHOA NELLIE! THE SLIPPERY SLOPE

*Ned Flanders' Illustrated Pocket Guide
to the 21 Danger Signs along
the Road to Moral Decay*

Catchy Pop Songs

Doncha Wanna Woogle?

Text Messaging

Bud3!
1 m s0
th3r3!!!

Spicy Cuisine

Aromatherapy

Open-Toed Shoes

Seat Warmers

Impulse Buys

YOUR HUSBAND...HE IS NOT HOME? YES?

Subtitles

Fast Forwarding

Plaids with Stripes

Casual Fridays

Cravings

Stimulants

Romance Novels

4-Ply Toilet Paper

Elastic Waistbands

Easy Outs

FEMA
NAFTA
BYOB
LOL
FAQ
NIMBY

Acronyms

Significant Others

The Internets

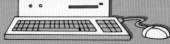

The Lyrical Stylin's of Ned Flanders

A Jaunty GENT OF ALL GENRES

FOUND MYSELF

by Ned "Hippity Hoppity" Flanders

You betcha I'm a poet, gosh doncha know it?
I got it, won't let it go willy-nilly
I've got this one darn dilly chance to show it
Tick tock! Opportunity knocks but once
Just one knock-adilly don't be silly
Access success like Milli Vanilli! Hi-dilly
Hi-diddily-ho neighboreeno
Of evil I speak hear or see no
I'm living la vida el cleano
I'm Mister Mellow, just a fellow
Who's tryin' to be nice—yo
Oppor-diddily-tunity won't ring twice—no
You only get one shot like Annie Oakely-dokily
One-dun-diddily shot so don't choke-ily-dokily
Might get booed by the throng, say Neddy don't belong
But I'm gonna sing my song anyhoodily-doodle
Tho I'm limp as a noodle, tho I'm a nervous Nellie
Got butterflies in my belly, my knees turn to jelly
Whew! I'm havin' a cow, I'm sh-shakin' in my Dockers
Lord don't fail me now, I see opportunity's knockers
Had my chance to show it, you know it, I didn't blow it
I bought it, I own it, won't be takin' it back to the store
I hear a rap at my door, it's a hip hop-portunity
Quoth the Nedster "Ever-diddily-more!"

nero's palace

by Ned "Funkadunkadoodle" Flanders

Her name was Amber. Or was it Ginger?
She worked in Vegas,
Serving cocktails at Nero's Palace.
She paid no taxes on her tips,
And wore makeup on her lips,
Like a floozy I once saw on "Dallas."
My spirits sinking, I started drinking,
I wasn't thinking...

At the Palace! At Nero's Palace!
I was in a nightspot in Las Vegas.
There at the Palace! At Nero's Palace!
Drunken passion is always in fashion
At the Palace...

Her name was Ginger. Or was it Amber?
I awoke in Vegas,
In a hot tub at Nero's Palace.
I had wed a waitress,
A cocktail waitress with a past.
One look and I sobered up fast.
The marriage was ill-fated, unconsummated,
We never even dated.

At the Palace! At Nero's Palace!
I was in a tight spot in Las Vegas.
I fled the Palace! Fled Nero's Palace!
Got her out of the picture, I just had to ditch her
At the Palace! At Nero's Palace!

ON FLANDERS' LAWN

by Ned "Folksy" Flanders

On Flanders' lawn the green grass grows
Sprinkily-dinkled by a hose,
But what demon seed lay in repose
On Flanders' lawn?

They are the weeds. The living dead,
"Ding-dang-diddly!" shouts out Ned,
"Skidaddily-doo!" And yet they spread
On Flanders' lawn.

Take up the battle, grab the hoe!
Whoa, Nellie! How fast they grow!
We'll fight all night 'til come the dawn.
We shall not sleep, lest more evil spawn.
On Flanders' lawn.

Yes, indeedily-weedily, it has come to blows.
There will be no peace, all Springfield knows,
'Til once again the green grass grows
On Flanders' lawn.

That's Life-a-ringy-a-dingy-ding-ding-doodle

Ned "Ol' Four Eyes" Flanders

Had a wife 'til the good Lord took her.
He brought her down
With an air-bazooka.
Now I'm missin' her meatloaf
And her low-fat apple strudel.
But that's life,
That's life-a-ringy-a-dingy-ding-ding-doodle.

I've been a winner, a loser, a lover, a liver,
A dad to Todd and to Rod.
I live next door to Homer Simpson,
And I still believe in God.
And each time I fe-fo-find myself down on my knees
I don't even ask, "Howdy-do, Lord, why me?"

No siree-bob! That's life,
And I won't dispute it.
Run it up the ol' flagdiddily-pole,
I'll stand and salute it.
That's life,
So darn pick-adilly fickle.
One day I'm thinkin' it ain't worth a silly nickel.
The next day I'm feelin' frisky
As a miniature poodle.
Because that's life,
That's life-a-ringy-a-dingy-ding-dang-doodle!

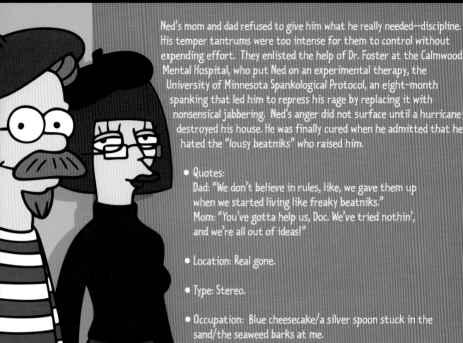

Ned's mom and dad refused to give him what he really needed—discipline. His temper tantrums were too intense for them to control without expending effort. They enlisted the help of Dr. Foster at the Calmwood Mental Hospital, who put Ned on an experimental therapy, the University of Minnesota Spankological Protocol, an eight-month spanking that led him to repress his rage by replacing it with nonsensical jabbering. Ned's anger did not surface until a hurricane destroyed his house. He was finally cured when he admitted that he hated the "lousy beatniks" who raised him.

- Quotes:
  Dad: "We don't believe in rules, like, we gave them up when we started living like freaky beatniks."
  Mom: "You've gotta help us, Doc. We've tried nothin', and we're all out of ideas!"

- Location: Real gone.

- Type: Stereo.

- Occupation: Blue cheesecake/a silver spoon stuck in the sand/the seaweed barks at me.

- Favorite foods: Naked lunch, reality sandwiches.

- Turn-ons: When Gene Krupa goes "boom boom... bah-bap-bap-bap, boom boom...bah-bap-bap-bap, boom boom boom...bah-bap-bap, bap-bah-bap, boom boom...tss!"

- Turn-offs: Rules, discipline, work, Ned.

- Burning for: The ancient heavenly connection to the starry dynamo in the machinery of night!

From the NEDitor in Chief
The Flanders Family Newsletter

Howdilly-diddily-doodily-do Fellow Flanderses,

Hope you all are di-diddily-doing okily-dokily! We menfolk here at Casa Flanderosa are doing fine and ding-dandy, yes indeedily-doodily!

...I'm home-schoolin' Rowdy Rod in ancient Greek... He wants to see for himself whether or not the Bible translation we use is absotively-posilutely correctomundo...

...Typhoon Todd reprised his role of Jesus in the Spring-field Christmas Pageant... Got us into a dilly of a pickle when I made the Toddster's costume from sheets left over from his bedwetting days... Gosharoonie! It's times like this when ol' Neddie sure misses the Mrs.!...

...As you know, we Flanderses love to meander, and so this year we hit the hi-diddily-highway and visited all 1,804 Applebee's de-diddily-licious restauroonies across these YOU-nited States of God Bless America... "Eatin' Scrumdiddily-umscious Good in the Flanders Hood!" That's our motto!...

...The Junior Campers organized a humdinger of a Cat Wash fundraiser to raise funds for next year's fundrais-ing drive...
The event was supposed to be a Car Wash, but due to an oopsie-whoopsie of the typographic-persuasion, we ended

up shampooin' a caboodle of clamorin', cantankerous kitties instead...

Never been one to toot my own horn, but (Beep! Beep!) yours truly has just been delegated to referee the finger-pointing at our upcoming Evergreen Terrace Home-owners Association Year-End Blame-a-Thon. Last year's group gripe took an unexpect-edly neighborly turn after an effigy of Homer Simpson was set on fire, and we all sang "Kumbaya"...

Hope I do-diddly-NOT sound like some kind of phony baloney name dropper, but my distinguished, extinguished Hollywood flame Sara Sloane has a new movie coming out: Pirates of the Hi-Carb Beerians... It's based on the "Little Land of Duff" ride at Duff Gardens. (Like Noah said as he was loading the Ark, "Now I herd every-thing!")... The movie is rated PU-13 (Purely Unwatchable for anyone over 13 years of age)... guess I'll just have to wait to see Sara in my G-rated dreams...

...Anyhoodily-doodle that's the up-diddily-date from Springfield...

Godspeed, Fellow Flanderses!

Ned

Ned's Christmas List

Hi-dilly-Ho-Ho-Ho, St. Nickety-Nick,

Besides the rootin'-tootin' Rapture, all I want
for Christmas—the holiest doodlin' day since All
Sainterinos' Day—is...
- Ziggy Archives, Vol. 10
- "Sweatin' to the Oldies" Vol. XVIII
  (VHS please!)
- Tax return forms
- Left-handed shoe buffer
- Left-handed taffy-puller
- Salt-resistant Bible for the boat
- Sheaves (for bringing in)
- Season pass to the Mt. Swartzwelder
  Historic Cider Mill
- 18-pack of Mt. Swartzwelder Historic Cider
- Newspaper shredder (I caught the Toddster
  reading "Dear Abby"!)

- Lip spinach trimmer
- Nose spinach trimmer
- Ear spinach trimmer
- Other spinach trimmer (in a plain brown wrapper)
- Green sweater
- Eyeglass wipes (with motivational sayings)
- Beatle boots
- MP3 Bible read aloud by Ryan Seacrest
- Piece of the True Cross (the one I have already is gettin' kinda shabby)
- Water-scented cologne
- Amazing Technicolor Dream Tie
- TV tray (borrowed by Homer)
- Weed whacker (borrowed by Homer)
- Upstairs bathtub (borrowed by Homer)
- A spare Jesus fish for the ol' Geo (in case Homer borrows one)

Thankily-dank you,
Steady Neddy

NED'S Bumper Stickers

 PRESBYLUTHERANISM

I'D RATHER BE DOWN ON MY KNEES
BEGGING THE LORD'S FORGIVENESS

Just Say Abso-NOT-ly
NO to NEGATIVITY

FRIENDS DON'T LET FRIENDS
BECOME MOVEMENTARIANS

University of Minnesota
Spankological Protocol Survivor

If This Geo's A-Rollin'
Let's Go Bowlin'

LITTLE PWAGMATTASQUARMESETTPORT
America's Scrod Basket

God Bless
SPRINGFIELD, USA

I'm Crazy for Calmwood!
CALMWOOD MENTAL HOSPITAL

 JH

WWND?

REAL MEN
Eat Plain Vanilla

got apple cider?

I BRAKE FOR JOGGERS,
BABY DUCKS, AND THE RAPTURE

★★★★★★★★★★★★★★★★★
REPUBLICAN-DO
★★★★★★★★★★★★★★★★★

Heaven Can Wait —
I'm Going to *Praiseland*

**TOO MANY BURGERS
NOT ENOUGH PROPANE**

I ♥ MY LEFT 🖐

FAITH, HOPE, OR CHARITY
No One Rides for Free

God Is My Co-Pilot, My Navigator,
and My Flight Attendant!

143

My Other Car is the
Wienermobile

Honk If You're RE-BORNY!

NED'S

1. BEATNIKS.
2. SATAN.
3. THE POST OFFICE.
4. SPANKINGS.
5. LEF-T-MART.
6. RED HOTS.
7. LOOSE CHANGE.
8. TIGHT ENDS.
9. WIDE RECEIVERS.
10. TINSELTOWN.
11. UNISEX CLOTHING.
12. INSULT COMIC DOGS.
13. FLYING NUNS.
14. TRANS FATS.
15. UNHAPPY CAMPERS.
16. IRONY.
17. CANADA.
18. BOB BALABAN.
19. HARRY POTTER.
20. CHARLES DARWIN.

BOTTOM 40